Corporate Personality
in Ancient Israel

Corporate Personality in Ancient Israel

H. WHEELER ROBINSON

Revised Edition

FORTRESS PRESS   PHILADELPHIA

"The Hebrew Conception of Corporate Personality" was first published in *Werden und Wesen des Alten Testaments: Vorträge gehalten auf der Internationalen Tagung Alttestamentlicher Forscher zu Göttingen vom 4.-10. September 1935,* ed. P. Volz, F. Stummer, and J. Hempel ("Beihefte zur Zeitschrift für die Alttestamentliche Wissenschaft," 66; Berlin, 1936), and is reprinted here by arrangement with the publisher, Alfred Töpelmann.

"The Group and the Individual in Israel" was first published in *The Individual in East and West* (ed. E. R. Hughes, 1937), and is here reprinted by arrangement with the publisher, Oxford University Press, Inc.

This book is a reissue of a volume originally published in 1964 by Fortress Press as part of *Facet Books, Biblical Series,* edited by John Reumann.

Second printing 1967
Revised edition 1980

Library of Congress Cataloging in Publication Data

Robinson, Henry Wheeler, 1872–1945.
    Corporate personality in ancient Israel.

    Bibliography: p.
    CONTENTS: The Hebrew conception of corporate personality.—The group and the individual in Israel.
        1. Jews—Social life and customs. 2. Social participation. I. Robinson, Henry Wheeler, 1872–1945. Group and the individual in Israel. 1980.
II. Title.
DS112.R7 1980   301.29'33   79–8887
ISBN 0–8006–1380–5

8019J79   Printed in the United States of America   1–1380

Contents

Introduction

It is not often that papers presented at professional conferences still deserve to be in print after some forty-five years, but the two articles which comprise this little volume are exceptions. There are several reasons why they should remain available to scholars and students. In the first place, H. Wheeler Robinson's views, especially as expressed in the chapter on corporate personality in ancient Israel, have been highly influential. Robinson speaks here for a generation and more of biblical scholarship. This work is, therefore, a significant chapter in the history of interpretation. Second, Robinson's essay continues to be important as one of the pioneering attempts to make use of anthropological theories and—to a lesser extent—anthropological data in the service of biblical interpretation. Finally, the articles in this volume should remain in print because the issues which they raise deserve—and are again receiving—the serious attention of biblical scholars.

In recent years debate has been renewed concerning the existence, meaning, and importance of a concept of corporate personality in ancient Israel. That discussion has arisen out of and then contributed to reflection upon major methodological questions concerning the relation of anthropology and sociology to biblical interpretation. On the one hand, in some circles the idea of corporate personality continues to be used almost uncritically.[1] That is, some seem to take it for granted that the concept is one of the assured results of biblical scholarship, and in turn use it in a variety of ways. In fact, some have used the concept as a foundation upon which to build theological structures.[2] On the other hand, according to some, by no means have all of Robinson's conclusions stood the test of time. Many of the views presented in these chapters may now appear quaint and outdated, and some are. Since the works first appeared in their American edition a number of scholars have mounted persuasive challenges to various aspects of Robinson's view of corporate personality. Both the use of and challenge to corporate personality suggest that the conclusions, the evidence for them, and the methods by which they were drawn should be reexamined at their source in the work of H. Wheeler Robinson.

Of the two chapters published here, the first has been the more influential and controversial. The basic notion that in ancient Israel there was a distinctive mentality in which the group could "function as a single individual through any one of those members conceived as representative of it" (p. 25) was mentioned in Robinson's works as early as 1911 but finds its fullest expression in the paper published here. The second paper, "The Group and the Individual in Israel," is in some ways a summary of Robinson's perspective on the history of the religion of Israel as found in works such as *The Religious Ideas of the Old Testament* and *Inspiration and Revelation in the Old Testament,* applied to the specific topic at hand and to the historical circumstances of 1936.

---

[1] See Rogerson's partial list in "The Hebrew Conception of Corporate Personality: A Re-Examination," *Journal of Theological Studies,* 21 (1970), 1, fn. 1.

[2] See C. Lattey, "Vicarious Solidarity in the Old Testament," *Vetus Testamentum,* 1 (1951), 267–74; E. C. Rust, *Nature and Man in Biblical Thought* (London: Lutterworth Press, 1953); and *idem, Salvation History* (Richmond: John Knox Press, 1962).

Robinson's "The Group and the Individual in Israel" has not drawn much specific attention in biblical criticism, but most of the framework which supported it has eroded away in recent decades. The chapter is an effort at a more or less sociological reconstruction of ancient Israel's life, for example, from nomadic to clan to town institutions. Like most of his contemporaries, Robinson saw consciousness of the individual emerging relatively late, and under the influence of the work of the classical prophets. The problem for him in this chapter was to show that the corporate consciousness was never quite lost. The framework for such an interpretation of Israel's development was the one which arose in the wake of Wellhausen's *Prolegomena to the History of Ancient Israel* (first published in 1878). Major elements of that reconstruction, including the view that the prophets introduced individualism, ethical monotheism, and spiritual religion, have been called into serious question by form-critical and traditio-historical investigation of the Old Testament. At the least, it must be said that the history of Israel's religion is far more complex than was believed before World War II. Likewise, new approaches to the social institutions and the social history of Israel are emerging, approaches which point toward very different reconstructions, for example, of the formative period of Israel's history in her land.[3]

If the second chapter of this book stresses sociology and history, the first focuses upon anthropology and psychology. Depending, as John Reumann points out in the introduction to the first American edition, upon the work of Johannes Pedersen,[4] and upon anthropological theories of

[3] See Norman K. Gottwald's *The Tribes of Yahweh: A Sociology of Liberated Israel, 1250–1050 B.C.E.* (Maryknoll, N.Y.: Orbis Books, 1979), and "Sociological Method in the Study of Ancient Israel," in Martin J. Buss, ed., *Encounter with the Text: Form and History in the Hebrew Bible*, "Semeia Supplements" (Missoula, Mont.: Scholars Press, and Philadelphia: Fortress Press, 1979), pp. 69–81.

[4] J. Pedersen, *Israel: its Life and Culture*, I–II (Copenhagen: Branner, and London: Oxford University Press, 1926), III–IV (1940).

his time, Robinson presented a very attractive picture of a distinctively Israelite view where the group and the individual were seen at points to merge. He then applied that view to a number of Old Testament texts.

One aspect of Robinson's theory was called into question by J. R. Porter.[5] Without raising fundamental questions about the concept as a whole, Porter inquired into the existence of a conception of corporate personality in Israelite law and juridical practice. He investigated the texts which Robinson used to argue for the presence of the notion in the realm of law (Josh. 7; II Sam. 21; Deut. 25:5–10; Deut. 21:1–9; Exod. 20:5; Deut. 5:9; Gen. 4:15, 24) and concluded that at most they have to do with corporate responsibility. That is, in some cases—and always for exceptional offenses which fall beyond the normal realm of law—the group may suffer for the offenses of an individual. He summarized his results as follows:

> It may be claimed that this concept [corporate personality] is prominent in hardly any of the examples as far as legal penalties are concerned, while other important aspects of Hebrew thinking are present in all. . . . What is debatable is how far Israelite law envisages the "psychic community" or the "psychical unity," the terms in which "corporate personality" has so commonly been defined. As far as the whole Hebrew legal system is concerned, there seems little reason to depart from the picture suggested by the Book of the Covenant that the law operated on the basis of the individual rather than the group . . .[6]

While Porter was unwilling to reject the possibility that an idea of corporate personality could have been operative in nonlegal contexts, it now seems clear that he had dealt a more serious blow to the theory than he indicated. Law, ethos, and the "mentality" of a culture go hand in hand.

---

[5] J. R. Porter, "Legal Aspects of Corporate Personality," *Vetus Testamentum* 15 (1965), 361–80.

[6] *Ibid.*, p. 379.

How important can a conception be which does not reflect itself in law and legal practice?

A far more comprehensive challenge was laid down by J. W. Rogerson in 1970.[7] Addressing himself to the matters which Porter had not considered, Rogerson noted that H. Wheeler Robinson had not adequately defined the term "corporate personality." That the term was vague explained in part the diverse uses to which it has been put over the years. Rogerson observed that the phrase appeared to have different meanings in Robinson's work, depending upon the context. For the most part, he concluded, corporate personality was used to denote two distinct things: "(i) corporate responsibility and (ii) a psychical unity between members of the same social group, in which the limits of an individual's personality are not clearly defined."[8] The first understanding meant that a member of a group could be held responsible for the action of the group. What Rogerson considered problematic about that view was Robinson's apparent assumption that such could be so because the member was not regarded as an individual. The second meaning carried the case a step further, depending upon "the inability of the individual clearly to recognize the limits of his own personality."[9]

It was this second—and to Robinson, more important —sense of corporate personality which depended so heavily upon current anthropological theories. As he acknowledged, Robinson was influenced by the work of L. Lévy-Bruhl,[10] who popularized the notion that primitive

---

[7] J. W. Rogerson, "The Hebrew Conception of Corporate Personality," *Journal of Theological Studies* 21 (1970), 1–16. See also his *Anthropology and the Old Testament* (Oxford: Basil Blackwell, and Atlanta: John Knox Press, 1979), especially pp. 55 ff.

[8] "The Hebrew Conception of Corporate Personality," p. 6.

[9] *Ibid.*, p. 7.

[10] *Primitive Mentality* (English trans. London, 1923); *How Natives Think* (English trans. London, 1926).

peoples have a mentality which is prelogical. Primitives were said to experience the world in a mystical way, not distinguishing between objects or between subjective and objective experiences.[11] As Rogerson has pointed out, Robinson assumed the validity of Lévy-Bruhl's theories and their applicability to ancient Israel. When prophets, for example, spoke of being in the heavenly court, or of their identification with God's voice, that was no figure of speech: they did not distinguish between visionary and ordinary experience.[12]

Among anthropologists, serious questions have been raised about the theories upon which H. Wheeler Robinson's view of corporate personality rested. Many have questioned the existence of a distinctive "mentality" among primitive peoples, as well as the use of materials from historically and geographically diverse cultures to establish such theories.[13] Likewise, biblical scholars have argued that often there are simpler explanations than corporate personality for many features of texts which Robinson explained in that way. Rogerson went so far as to conclude, "It seems to me that the onus is upon scholars who continue to talk of corporate personality to define what they mean, and to say upon what it is based if it implies a Hebrew mentality different from our own."[14] In view of developments in both anthropology and biblical studies,[15] Rogerson's admonitions should be taken with utmost seriousness.

Nevertheless, one must still give account of the views of Old Testament texts—not to say Israelite mentality—

[11] Rogerson, "The Hebrew Conception of Corporate Personality," p. 7.

[12] *Ibid.*, pp. 7–8; Rogerson, *Anthropology and the Old Testament*, p. 56.

[13] Rogerson, *Anthropology and the Old Testament*, pp. 46–65.

[14] *Ibid.*, pp. 56–57.

[15] See especially the frontal attacks on the idea of a distinctive Hebrew mentality in the works of James Barr, e.g., *The Semantics of Biblical Language* (Oxford: Oxford University Press, 1961) and *Biblical Words for Time*, "Studies in Biblical Theology," No. 33 (London: SCM, 1962).

concerning the individual and the group, the person and the community. Few will doubt that according to many preexilic prophetic announcements the nation as a whole is judged on the basis of the sins of some, or that according to the Deuteronomistic historian (Deut. through II Kings) the king could bring the wrath of Yahweh upon the whole people, or that according to some traditions "the sins of the fathers are visited upon the children to the seventh generation." Such expressions need not be explained by recourse to a "psychical unity" of individual and group.

That the social-institutional dimensions of existence were of great importance in ancient Israel must be stressed. Further, the particular Old Testament expressions of the awareness of the interdependence of human life in society must be examined. Such an examination is among the goals of the renewed sociological—and anthropological—investigation of ancient Israel.

GENE M. TUCKER

Emory University
Atlanta
November 1979

Introduction to the
First Edition

Few topics have come to pervade modern biblical studies as has the Hebrew conception of "corporate personality." The classic (and pioneer) presentation of this topic is a paper read in 1935 by the British Baptist scholar H. Wheeler Robinson. Though published in English and frequently referred to, the essay has not been widely read, perhaps because it originally appeared in Germany in a rather inaccessible volume, which was printed as a supplement to a learned journal. Facet Books now makes this important article available to a wider audience, and with it another, more popular but even lesser known lecture delivered by the same author in 1936, "The Group and the Individual in Israel." Together the two provide an excellent introduction to that important Semitic complex of thought in which there is a constant oscillation between the individual and the group—family, tribe, or nation—to which he belongs, so that the king or some other representative figure may be said to embody the group, or the group may be said to sum up the host of individuals.

15

The author of these two essays, Henry Wheeler Robinson, is almost as intriguing as the topic he treats. Born on February 7, 1872, at Northampton in central England, he was raised by his mother and at the age of fifteen had to leave school to go to work in the countinghouse of a Northampton leather merchant. After his baptism in 1888, he distinguished himself as a Sunday school teacher, and soon he preached his first sermon. He continued to study in evening classes and began to contribute articles to a local Nonconformist magazine. Encouraged by friends, in 1890 he entered Regent's Park College, the Baptist training school in London, to study for the ministry.

Ten years of study followed, in London, at Edinburgh University (1891–95), then at Mansfield College, the Congregational theological school in Oxford, and at the continental universities of Marburg and Strassburg, where young Robinson attended the classes of such Old Testament scholars as Karl Budde and Theodor Nöldeke. He had shown special ability in Semitic studies, and while at Mansfield College, where he worked particularly under George Buchanan Gray, he was awarded several prizes, especially for his work on terms in Hebrew psychology.

Setting academic promise aside, he accepted a call to a Baptist congregation at Pitlochry, Scotland, where he settled with his bride in 1900. In 1903 he was persuaded to move to St. Michael's Baptist Church in Coventry, a difficult situation which demanded sturdy faith as well as decided tact; nonetheless in his three years there membership in the small congregation rose substantially. During these years in the parish, Robinson showed himself a careful preacher, an exacting teacher, and a dedicated scholar. His midweek services and Sunday Bible classes brought teaching opportunities at which he lectured on an astonishing range of topics; out of one such series of lectures grew his later book *The Cross of Job.*

In 1906 Robinson was called to Rawdon Baptist College, outside Leeds, where he at first taught almost everything except Old Testament. By 1914, in addition to his college duties, he was lecturing at the University of Leeds. During the wartime emergency in 1917, he added to his already considerable burdens by assuming charge of a local congregation. Nevertheless a steady stream of books and articles issued from his pen during these years. There were commentaries on Deuteronomy and Joshua (in the *Century Bible*, 1907), Jeremiah, Obadiah, and Micah (in *Peake's Commentary*, 1919), and articles for the *Encyclopaedia Britannica's* famed eleventh edition (1910), Hastings' *Dictionary of the Apostolic Church*, and Hastings' *Encyclopaedia of Religion and Ethics*. He produced the first edition of his *The Christian Doctrine of Man* (1911); a book, still in print, on *The Religious Ideas of the Old Testament* (1913); numerous articles in denominational papers; and a treatise on Baptist principles that was later translated into German and Danish. To carry this work load he arose at 5 A.M., tutored his children before breakfast, and often ended the day in his study at 2 A.M. It is small wonder that such labors drove his body to a near fatal collapse in 1913. But out of the ordeal of illness came a concern for the meaning of suffering which was to be reflected in several books, beginning with *The Cross of Job* (1916). There emerged too an ever increasing interest in the work of the Holy Spirit. It is characteristic of Wheeler Robinson's approach that before publishing his famous book on the Holy Spirit he set up a plan that supplemented scholarly analysis of biblical texts with group experience. He invited six friends to join him in an experimental seminar which called for half a year's preliminary study of a syllabus on the topic of the Holy Spirit followed by sessions that involved the participants in corporate devotions and reflections on their own Christian experience. Later Robinson took advantage of the corporate thinking offered in sessions with pastoral associations to develop further his theology of the Spirit.

New demands on Robinson's time came when he was elected Principal of Regent's Park College in 1920. Here he was able to fulfill a dream from his own student days of locating a Baptist theological college in the environment of one of Britain's two great universities. In 1926 the decision was made to move Regent's Park College to Oxford. The Old Testament scholar now found himself not only an administrator but also a fund-raiser, and that in the depths of a depression. Although he and his family moved to Oxford in 1927, for ten years he commuted between there and London, teaching at both places until 1938 when the cornerstone was laid for the new Regent's Park College, construction of which was opportunely completed just as World War II began. In the opinion of his biographer, Ernest Payne, the college in Oxford will always be H. Wheeler Robinson's "chief memorial."

Once again Robinson's many duties did not diminish his literary output. An essay published in 1925 testified to his continuing interest in Hebrew psychology, and a book on Baptist history published in 1927 reflected his role as a leader in his church and as president of the Baptist Historical Society. Lectures on "The Cross of Jeremiah" and "The Cross of the Servant" were published in 1925 and 1926 respectively, and a further volume on the problem of suffering in 1939. His book on the Holy Spirit appeared in 1928, a dozen years after the experimental seminar. An intensely personal book in the sphere of devotional literature, *The Veil of God,* came out in 1936. His many contributions to Old Testament study included *The History of Israel,* which was published in 1938 and is still being reprinted. Robinson's interest in systematic theology is evidenced in his last two books, *Redemption and Revelation in the Actuality of History* (1942) and *Inspiration and Revelation in the Old Testa-*

ment (published posthumously in 1946). The former book may be said to be the climax of Robinson's great trilogy consisting of *The Christian Doctrine of Man* (1911), *The Christian Experience of the Holy Spirit* (1928), and *Redemption and Revelation* (1942).

Editorial work also claimed much of Robinson's time. Between 1927 and 1942 fifteen volumes in the "Library of Constructive Theology" (of which he was coeditor) passed over his desk. For the two symposia which he edited, *Record and Revelation* (1938) and *The Bible in Its Ancient and English Versions* (1940), he also provided significant essays. *Record and Revelation* was undertaken for the British Society for Old Testament Study, of which he was a past president.

Solid learning, wide intellectual interests, deep piety— these are the traits remembered by Robinson's students and associates. A man with a fantastic zeal for work, he took few vacations, although he did enjoy reading detective stories, a passion shared by many other theologians. He early realized the potentialities of religious broadcasting, then in its infancy, and spoke on the radio on more than one occasion. Christians beyond his own communion knew him not only through his writings but also through his participation in the ecumenical movement; church unity, he believed, would best be shown at the Lord's table and in the Spirit's work. Robinson is said to have made some of his deepest personal impressions on students through his Saturday morning sermon classes and through the Friday evening communion services which he instituted at Regent's Park College. In 1942, on his seventieth birthday, he was honored with a volume of essays by his former pupils and colleagues, and that spring retired from the college. Though he continued to lecture at Oxford and elsewhere, in the three years that remained of his retirement failing health precluded the realization of some of his fondest dreams, including a projected theology of the Old Testament. He died on May 12, 1945, three days after the end of the war in Europe.

What concerns us here in the work of Wheeler Robinson is the development of his understanding of corporate personality. During his student days at Mansfield College he had written an essay on Hebrew psychology for George Buchanan Gray, which he later expanded into a dissertation on "The Psychological Terms of the Hebrews"; this dissertation, submitted while he was at Pitlochry, won Robinson the Senior Kennicott Hebrew Scholarship at Oxford in 1901. Out of this study grew the paper on "Hebrew Psychology in Relation to Pauline Anthropology" which he contributed in 1908 to the volume of *Mansfield College Essays* honoring A. M. Fairbairn. Fairbairn (1838–1912), a noted Congregationalist theologian, had encouraged and furthered Robinson's career at several points; Robinson's essay in his honor opened up new aspects in biblical and theological investigation. It contains *in nuce* some of the ideas later developed in the two essays printed here and, though many of its points are now commonplaces of biblical study, it ought to be read as background to these essays.

In the essay honoring Fairbairn, Robinson sought to show that "Paul, a Hebrew of the Hebrews, is primarily and characteristically Hebrew in his anthropology, and that even where his ideas (in this realm) come nearest to a Greek form or are clothed in a Greek terminology, they are a legitimate outcome of Old Testament conceptions" (p. 268). Such a Hebraic background of Pauline theology is by now widely conceded, but in a period when Paul was being interpreted almost exclusively in light of Greek mystery cults, Wheeler Robinson was striking a new note. He carefully analyzed Old Testament terms like "soul" *(nephesh)* and "spirit" *(ruach),* and then showed how Paul uses Greek words to express an essentially Hebraic anthropology.

Ideas which reappear in a more developed form in Robinson's later writings are broached here: that animism stands behind Hebrew psychology; that man is no "immortal soul imprisoned in a body" but an interreaction of "breathsoul," spirit, and the body with its various organs, that he is in short "an animated body," to use the phrase that Robinson employed later; and that the Christian is essentially the product of the divine Spirit to whom he has yielded himself. The essay concluded that the trunk of Pauline anthropology is formed by Hebrew psychology and that, although Paul transforms each Old Testament concept, he does so without taking grafts from Hellenism (p. 285).

These lines of thought, only sketchily stated in 1909, are worked out in more detail in later articles, notably in the several editions of *The Christian Doctrine of Man* and in an essay on "Hebrew Psychology" published in 1925. The first essay in this Facet Book represents the real flowering of these years of investigation. It was read to the Second International Congress of Old Testament Scholars at Göttingen in September 1935. Robinson had had ties with German biblical scholarship ever since his student days, and after World War I was chosen as the representative of British scholarship to contribute a paper to the German periodical *Zeitschrift für die alttestamentliche Wissenschaft,* and thus to help reestablish the ties the war had severed. The Congress in 1935 attracted some eighty-five biblical scholars, including such luminaries as Alt, von Rad, Baumgärtel, Augustin Bea (the future Cardinal), Eissfeldt, Weiser, Rowley, and T. H. Robinson. In this galaxy Wheeler Robinson's address stood out nonetheless. Johannes Hempel remarked that it was "for many of us an advance into a new land" (*Zeitschrift für die alttestamentliche Wissenschaft,* XII [1935], 303), although Robinson admittedly built on much that he had said previously as well as on the work of

Johannes Pedersen in Denmark and the parallel but independent investigations of Otto Eissfeldt (cf. p. 41, n. 63 below).

The following year Robinson was asked to participate in a lecture series for Oxford undergraduates on the individual in various societies. His presentation on "The Group and the Individual in Israel," published in an anthology in 1937 and reprinted here, thus appeared in the broader setting of study of the individual in primitive society, Chinese thought, Hinduism, and so forth. The change of audience accounts for the absence of Hebrew terms, the dearth of scholarly apparatus, and the more far-reaching allusions. The setting also accounts for the fact that Robinson addresses himself at the close to the bearing which his study had on the present-day world, something all the lecturers were asked to do; hence also the care with which Robinson, in the world of 1936, distinguished "corporate personality" from "collectivism." It is noteworthy, however, that in a series on the individual Robinson begins with the primary place of the group; this is true to his societary emphasis. However, the very theme of the individual compels him to state in more detail and with greater clarity what he had noted as point "4" of his 1935 essay but had not developed there, since he regarded it as something obvious to the professional scholars of that day. Since the later essay, on "group and individual," gives a more balanced picture of the whole subject, it might well be read first, especially if the pages on "corporate personality" prove too intricate at first reading. It is in the 1935 address to Old Testament scholars, however, that the more careful foundations are laid.

Since 1936, of course, debate about Wheeler Robinson's theses on the group and the individual has continued. His own books, notably *Redemption and Revelation* and *Inspiration and Revelation,* often allude to the conception. Edmond Jacob has rightly called his essay a "classical formulation," but agreement has not been total by any means. Of the specific applications which Robinson suggested in 1935, that involving the figure of the Servant in Deutero-Isaiah has been especially debated. Robinson had suggested that the long dispute over whether "the Servant" is some historical individual or represents instead the nation Israel might be resolved by recognizing the oscillations of corporate personality. While some sort of "collective theory," usually associated with this concept of personality, seems the most attractive view today (according to the surveys of C. R. North), it must be added that scholars of the Scandinavian school, such as Lindblom and Engnell, who approach such problems in light of the community and its cult and of a king and future Messiah figure, make little use of the corporate personality theory. Other scholars, like Eichrodt, believe that an individual is intended.

With regard to Robinson's application of corporate personality to the use of the pronoun "I" in the Psalms—a problem long debated by the exegetes—it must be confessed that recent discussion of such psalms by no means agrees that an application of the corporate personality idea solves the problem. In his commentary on the Psalms Artur Weiser returns to the view set forth by Balla in 1912 that the "I" of individual laments does refer to an individual person and not to the community speaking with a single voice; Weiser adds, however, that the individual speaks in the context of the cult of the covenant festival, so that the "I" is not to be interpreted in terms of modern individualistic piety.

In New Testament study there have been other applications of corporate personality, often along lines hinted at by Robinson. T. W. Manson, for example, makes use of the concept of corporate personality in explaining some of the "Son of man" sayings in the Gospels; the "church" or "people of God" theme is implicit in Jesus' teachings, says

Manson. And one of the possible backgrounds of the Pauline concept of the church as "the body of Christ" continues to be the corporate personality idea.

Both essays are here reprinted very much as Robinson first published them. A few obvious misprints have been corrected, punctuation and capitalization have been altered to conform to American usage, the footnotes have been numbered consecutively for each essay, and the Hebrew words have been transliterated according to the system employed in Pedersen's *Israel,* a book which Robinson quotes several times in the first essay. The bibliographical information in Robinson's footnotes is often scanty; thirty years after the publication of the essays it is necessary to identify more fully works which were familiar to Robinson's fellow scholars. This information has been supplied by the editor. The translations appearing in brackets have also been provided by the editor, as has other material that appears in brackets. All biblical quotations seem to be cited either from the Revised Version of 1881–85 or in Robinson's own translation; they have been left in their original form. In some cases such quotations of course agree with the King James Version or, strikingly, anticipate the Revised Standard Version.

Full bibliographical data for all titles noted in this Introduction will be found at the end of the book in the section "For Further Reading."

JOHN REUMANN

Lutheran Theological Seminary
Philadelphia
March 1964

The Hebrew Conception
of Corporate Personality

In the terminology of English law, "corporation" denotes either "a body corporate legally authorized to act as a single individual," or "an artificial person created by royal charter, prescription, or legislative act, and having the capacity of perpetual succession."[1] Both usages are covered by the Hebrew conception of corporate personality, though without the necessity for any legal prescription. The larger or smaller group was accepted without question as a unity; legal prescription was replaced by the fact or fiction of the blood-tie, usually traced back to a common ancestor. The whole group, including its past, present, and future members, might function as a single individual through any one of those members conceived as representative of it. Because it was not confined to the living, but included the dead and the unborn, the group could be conceived as living forever.

No one can overlook this unity of corporate personality in its more legal aspects. Familiar examples from the Old

[1] *Shorter Oxford English Dictionary, s.v.*

Testament are given when Achan breaks the taboo on the spoil of Jericho, and involves the whole of Israel in defeat and, on discovery, the whole of his family in destruction;[2] or when seven of Saul's descendants are executed to expiate the Gibeonite blood shed by Saul;[3] or in the practice of Levirate marriage, which (on any explanation of its origin) points to a unitary group conception;[4] or in the responsibility of a whole city for murder or heathenism within its area;[5] or in the belief that Yahweh visits the iniquities of the fathers upon the children;[6] or in the practices of the blood-feud, before it was limited by the *lex talionis*.[7] Such examples are very familiar. They have to be admitted because they found expression in external acts. They presuppose a conception of the family or clan very different from the group ideas of today. The modern man usually starts from the rights of the individual; English law, for example, warrants the removal of the child from the control of the father, where its individual claims are at stake.[8] This, of course, is in direct opposition to the ancient *patria potestas;*[9] in modern times a son might feel morally bound to pay his father's debts, but in the ancient world he would often have been sold as a slave to pay them.

It is, however, not only in Hebrew law that the conception operates, but also in ways much less easy to detect, because

---

[2] Josh. 7. Such social solidarity is found throughout the world wherever there is a primitive but socially organized group; cf. A. H. Post, *Afrikanische Jurisprudenz*, p. 49. For other examples see M. Löhr, *Sozialismus und Individualismus im Alten Testament* (Giessen, 1906), *passim;* Otto Procksch, *Über die Blutrache bei den vorislamischen Arabern* (Leipzig, 1899).

[3] II Sam. 21.

[4] Deut. 25:5 ff.; cf. J. M. Mittelmann, *Der altisraelitische Levirat* (Leipzig, 1934), p. 7.

[5] Deut. 13:12 ff., 21:1 ff.

[6] Exod. 20:5.

[7] Gen. 4:15, 24; Exod. 21:23–25.

[8] *Encyclopaedia Britannica, s.v.* "Children-Protective Laws." The Children Act was passed in 1908.

[9] Judg. 11:34 ff.; Jer. 32:35; Deut. 21:18 ff., etc.

they have found less open expression. They are often important for the exegesis of the Old Testament, and will be illustrated in the second part of this paper. But it is necessary first to glance at certain aspects of the conception itself. Four of these call for special notice, viz., (1) the unity of its extension both into the past and into the future; (2) the characteristic "realism" of the conception, which distinguishes it from "personification," and makes the group a real entity actualized in its members; (3) the fluidity of reference, facilitating rapid and unmarked transitions from the one to the many, and from the many to the one; (4) the maintenance of the corporate idea even after the development of a new individualistic emphasis within it.

(1) The extension of the living family to include its ancestors, or, as we should rather say, the extension of the ancestors to include the living members of the family, is best expressed in the familiar phrases about being gathered to one's fathers, or going to one's fathers, or to one's kindred.[10] Thus Jacob says, "I am to be gathered unto my kindred; bury me with my fathers" (Gen. 49:29). This shows that burial in the family sepulcher is the realistic act which unites a man with his ancestors. If he is not properly buried, this unity is not properly achieved. No doubt it is difficult for us to reconcile this burial in a grave with the conception of Sheol, except by thinking of Sheol as an assemblage of all the graves. Thus in Ezekiel (32:17-32), the shades of Sheol are depicted in groups according to different nationalities and fortunes. Yet as Pedersen[11] reminds us, Sheol is not the mere sum of the separate graves. "All graves have certain common characteristics constituting the nature of the grave, and that is Sheol. The 'Ur'-grave we

---

[10] Gen. 15:15, 25:8, 49:29; Num. 27:13.

[11] J. Pedersen, *Israel: its Life and Culture*, I–II (Copenhagen: Branner, and London: Oxford University Press, 1926), p. 462.

might call Sheol; it belongs deep down under the earth, but it manifests itself in every single grave as *mō'abh* manifests itself in every single Moabite. Where there is grave, there is Sheol, and where there is Sheol, there is grave." We notice also that both Samuel and Joab are buried in their own houses.[12] This illustrates the common belief that the ghost remained in specially close relation to the grave in which the body had been buried.[13]

There is a similar extension of the living group into the future as part of its unity. This is best illustrated by the dominant aspiration of the Hebrew to have male children to perpetuate his name, the name that was so much part of himself that something of him died when his name ceased. It was as much of a misfortune to have no male children as to miss the proper burial rites. "Man is only what he is as a link in the family."[14] Thus what Robertson Smith has said of the living group may be extended both before and after. "A kin was a group of persons whose lives were so bound up together, in what must be called a physical unity, that they could be treated as parts of one common life. The members of one kindred looked on themselves as one living whole, a single animated mass of blood, flesh and bones, of which no member could be touched without all the members suffering."[15]

Along such lines, then, the corporate personality of the family, the clan, and the people was conceived realistically as a unity, a unity which made possible the all-important doctrine of election, and lent unity to the history itself. Amos can address his contemporaries in the eighth century as still "the whole family which I brought up out of the land

---

[12] I Sam. 25:1; I Kings 2:34.

[13] E.g., Rachel, Jer. 31:15 (cf. I Sam. 10:2).

[14] Pedersen, *op. cit.,* p. 259. Cf. II Sam. 14:7.

[15] W. Robertson Smith, *Lectures on the Religion of the Semites* (new ed., rev.; London: A. and C. Black, 1894), pp. 273–74. We may compare Isa. 58:7, "hide not thyself from thine own flesh," and Rom. 11:14, where Paul speaks of the Jews as "my flesh."

of Egypt,"[16] since they are both its representatives and its actual constituents. The people *are* their ancestors, as the patriarchal narratives often illustrate. The conception of history as a unity derives in the last resort through Christianity from the Hebrew prophets and apocalyptists, and they are working with the unity of corporate personality. We may still speak of the unity of a nation's history, but we mean something very different from the ancient concrete conception. *We* mean the immanent evolution of its characteristic; *they* meant that concrete realism which has been exhibited.

(2) This realism is itself a second characteristic point of difference between ancient and modern ideas. The Hebrew conception is neither a literary personification nor an ideal. Its study does not belong to the linguistic, but to the archaeological and anthropological sides of the subject. It is an instinctive and not a consciously made unification. Pedersen brings that out forcibly when he speaks of the individual Moabite *(mō'abhi)* as a manifestation of the type *(mō'abh)*, "which is the sum and substance of Moabitic features," acting as a unity and treated as such.[17] In the light of such considerations, a deeper meaning is given to the detailed individualistic portraiture of such passages as describe the national history through the life-story of an unchaste woman in Ezekiel 16 and 23,[18] or through that of a forsaken and barren but now restored wife, the mother of many children, in Isaiah 54:1 ff. An impressive example is afforded by the passage in Daniel 7:13, 27, where the human figure coming with the clouds of heaven is explicitly identified as the people of the saints of the Most High. This

---

[16] Amos 3:1.

[17] *Op. cit.,* p. 109.

[18] Eissfeldt points out that the individualizing traits here go beyond anything we find in the description of the Servant of Yahweh *(Einleitung in das Alte Testament* [Tübingen: J. C. B. Mohr, 1934], p. 382; 2nd ed. [1956], p. 412).

means that their unity is so realistically conceived that it can be concentrated into a single representative figure. If we ask on what this unity is based, the answer for the Semites at least is doubtless that of the common blood-tie, whether real or fictitious (as by a blood covenant or some form of adoption), rather than of the cult of a common ancestor—though this itself also expresses the unity. But quite definitely we must *not* think of anything like Rousseau's rights of man and voluntary social contract. Nor must we think of a merely ideal or figurative existence of Rachel, when the prophet depicts her as weeping for her children by the family graves;[19] Rachel weeps because she dies in her children. Still further, we must note the relation of this conception of corporate personality to that of individual personality, as shown by the psychological ideas of the Hebrews. For them, the personality consisted of a number of bodily organs animated by a breath-soul and each possessing a diffused and distributed psychical and ethical quality. It is precisely the same idea which belongs to the unity of the group. The group possesses a consciousness which is distributed amongst its individual members and does not exist simply as a figure of speech or as an ideal. Indeed we may generalize to the extent of saying that there is usually a close parallelism between the psychology of the individual and the conception of society which prevails in any age. We may see it in Plato's *Republic,* through his close comparison of the individual and the state.[20] We may see it in the Pauline description of the church[21] as the "body of Christ." We may see it also in the biological ideas of modern times as applied both to the individual and to the social organism. Perhaps it

---

[19] Jer. 31:15.

[20] *Republic*, ii. 369: "the counterpart of the greater as it exists in the form of the less"; iv. 435: "there exist in each of us the same generic parts and characteristics as are found in the state" (Eng. trans. by Davies and Vaughan).

[21] I Cor. 12:12 ff. Cf. *Ep. ad Diognetum,* 6: "The soul is spread through all the members of the body."

is inevitable, since the only unity we can know directly is that of our own consciousness, so that our way of conceiving this will always tend to be reflected in our view of society.

(3) The fluidity of transition from the individual to the society and *vice versa* can be most easily illustrated from levels of consciousness far below those of the Old Testament, and especially from totemistic groups. (These more primitive conceptions have, of course, been sublimated in the Old Testament ideas, like the taboo-conception of holiness, or like the symbolic magic which underlies the symbolic acts of the prophets.) The group conception in primitive thought has been specially studied by Lévy-Bruhl[22] and by Durkheim,[23] in relation to the Australian aborigines. The former writer calls this conception "the law of participation," by which he means that "things, beings, and phenomena can be in a manner incomprehensible for us, at once themselves and something other than themselves."[24] This quasi-mystical identification he notes as one of the outstanding characteristics of prelogical mentality. "It permits the primitive mind to think at the same time of the individual in the collective and the collective in the individual."[25] "Each individual *is* at one and the same time such and such a man, or such and such a woman, actually alive, such an ancestral individual (human or semihuman) who lived in the mythical times of the *Alcheringa*, and at the same time he *is* his totem, i.e., he participates mystically in the essence of the animal or vegetable species of which he bears the name."[26] It is not suggested that the Hebrews passed

[22] *Les Fonctions Mentales dans les Sociétés Inférieures* (1910), Eng. trans. L. A. Clare, *How Natives Think* (New York: Knopf, 1926).

[23] *Les Formes Élémentaires de la Vie Religieuse* (Paris, 1912), Eng. trans. Joseph Ward Swain, *The Elementary Forms of the Religious Life* (London: G. Allen and Unwin, and New York: Macmillan, 1915).

[24] *Les Fonctions Mentales*, p. 77.

[25] *Ibid.*, p. 100.

[26] *Ibid.*, p. 94; cf. Durkheim, *Les Formes Élémentaires*, pp. 336 ff.

through such a totemistic stage, but simply that such absence of the sharp antitheses familiar to us is psychologically possible. But if so, then transitions from the one to the many and from the many to the one were much easier for them than for us.

We may illustrate the same kind of transition, worked out in a long development, from the religion of the ancient Egyptians. Wolf[27] has recently suggested that the absence of a consciousness of sin and the need of redemption, in spite of the Osirian judgment of the dead, is due to the absence of self-conscious individuality. It was the people as a whole, represented by the divine king, who had to do with God. Only when absolute kingship replaced representative kingship, toward the end of the Middle Kingdom, was there sufficient disintegration for more direct relation of the individual with Osiris; but then the religion possessed no creative force. The parallel and contrast with Israel's development of individualism is obvious, for there the transition led to the richest development of the religion. In all the generations there is this interplay of sociality and individuality, for they both belong essentially to our human nature. But in the ancient world they were much more closely and subtly blended than in the more self-conscious modern, and so it was possible to combine both, or to pass easily from one to the other.

(4) In accordance with this general principle, it is quite wrong to place the individualism of Jeremiah and Ezekiel in direct antithesis to the group conception which had hitherto prevailed. The group conception still remained dominant, notwithstanding the extreme consequences as to moral and religious responsibility which Ezekiel draws from his individualistic emphasis;[28] we have only to think of

[27] Walther Wolf, *Individuum und Gemeinschaft in der ägyptischen Kultur,* pp. 17–21.
[28] Ezek. 18.

his vision of a restored and regenerated community[29] to see this. So with his forerunner Jeremiah. The prophecy of the New Covenant[30] stands for the multiplication of the prophet's own consciousness of God, when all the Lord's people shall be prophets; yet it is a covenant with Israel as a nation, like the old covenant, however different its method. The later development of the eschatology shows that the complete destiny of the individual can be realized only if the nation accomplishes its own.[31] In the later Judaism, as Moore points out,[32] "'a lot in the World to Come' . . . is ultimately assured to every Israelite on the ground of the original election of the people by the free grace of God." The individualizing development takes place within the matrix of a social relation to God.[33] On the other hand, it is equally wrong to emphasize the social relation in the earlier period to the point of neglecting the fact of individual religion and morality. It must have been true that the earlier prophets, addressing Israel as a nation, and challenging it to repentance, or even simply condemning its sins, were in some degree thinking in terms of the individual Israelite. In fact, as we have just seen from Jeremiah, the new individualism was a product of the individual religious experience of the prophets, which must inevitably lead them to individualize within the collective mass which they formally addressed. This must have been reinforced by the response of their disciples, itself creating a new group within the

[29] Chaps. 37 and 40 ff.

[30] Jer. 31:33–34; cf. (at a lower level) Num. 11:29; Joel 3:1–2 [in Eng. trans., Joel 2:28–29].

[31] Adolphe Lods, Les prophètes d'Israël et les débuts du judaisme (Paris, 1935), p. 375; Eng. trans. S. H. Hooke, The Prophets of Israel and the Rise of Judaism (London: Routledge and Kegan Paul, 1937), p. 331.

[32] George Foot Moore, Judaism in the First Centuries of the Christian Era: The Age of the Tannaim (Cambridge: Harvard University Press, 1927–30), II, 94–95.

[33] Even the late individualism of Job passes easily into the universal experience of suffering, and shows what Eissfeldt calls die kollektivistische Verhaftung des jüdischen Individuums ["the confining of the individual in Judaism within the collective"] (Einleitung in das Alte Testament, op. cit., p. 516; 2nd ed., p. 571).

larger unit, and prophesying a new Israel.[34] But even so, the prophets are not to be assimilated to the journalist, the politician, and the preacher of today, addressing individuals in order to form a new community within state or church. The prophets always worked within the larger unity of Israel, and from Israel in the mass toward Israel as found in its most worthily representative Israelites.

So far, we have considered the more general aspects of the conception of corporate personality, and it has been suggested that this affects the whole relation of Israelites to one another and to Yahweh. It is, of course, impossible to attempt any exhaustive review of its applications. They would range from the accidence and syntax of Hebrew grammar up to the highest levels of Old Testament theology. It is not fanciful to see the collective emphasis in the apparent priority of collective nouns to those which represent units (cf. c̄ōn, ["flock"], and seh, ["one of a flock"]),[35] in the unity of idea which underlies the use of the construct state, and in the use of such words as nephesh ["breath," "spirit," or "soul"], lēbh ["heart"], dām ["blood"] in the singular with plural suffixes.[36] On the other hand, the fundamental conception of the covenant (berîth), which can be made the basis of a complete theology of the Old Testament,[37] is inseparably linked to the conception of corporate personality. For our present purpose, however, it must

[34] Isa. 8:16; cf. Mal. 3:16–17.

[35] Carl Brockelmann, Kurzgefasste vergleichende Grammatik der semitischen Sprachen ("Porta Linguarum Orientalium," 21; Berlin: Reuther and Reichard, 1908), p. 209.

[36] Cf. W. Robertson Smith, Kinship and Marriage in Early Arabia (Cambridge University Press, 1885), p. 40: "The whole kindred conceives itself as having a single life, just as in the formula 'our blood has been spilt' it speaks of itself as having but one blood in its veins."

[37] As by Walther Eichrodt, in his very useful Theologie des Alten Testaments; 3 parts (Leipzig: J. C. Hinrichs, 1933–39); trans. J. A. Baker from the 6th German ed. (1959), Theology of the Old Testament, Volume One ("The Old Testament Library"; Philadelphia: Westminster, 1961).

suffice to select three outstanding types of application, all of great and wide importance for exegesis, viz., (1) the representation of the nation by some outstanding figure belonging to it; (2) the individual-collective nature of the "I" of the Psalms and of the "Songs of the Servant of Yahweh"; (3) the character and content of Hebrew morality as the right relation of individual members of the group to one another.

(1) In the first place, the conception throws light on the peculiar prominence of individual personalities both in the making of Hebrew history and in the development of Hebrew religion.[38] At first sight, this may seem a paradox, when we are stressing the community sense. Yet it is a paradox only in appearance. Where the corporate sense is strong, the outstanding man will gather to himself the force of the whole group. Thus T. E. Lawrence can say of modern Bedouins, "Among the Arabs there were no distinctions, traditional or natural, except the unconscious power given a famous sheikh by virtue of his accomplishment," whilst in another place he can characterize the Semites as "the race of the individual genius."[39] In the patriarchal narratives of Genesis the great ancestors of Israel, Abraham, Isaac, and Jacob, are a remarkable blend of the typical Israelite with the nation, and thus fittingly its representatives, since as S. A. Cook remarks, "Hebrew thought refers with equal facility to a representative individual or to the group he represents."[40] When the monarchy emerges, the king is Yahweh's son, which is exactly what Hosea calls the nation.[41] The king represents the people to Yahweh; he was, in C. R. North's words, "a Priest in and through whom the people were brought near to God, rather than a Prophet

---

[38] H. Wheeler Robinson, *The Religious Ideas of the Old Testament* (London: Duckworth, 1913), pp. 20–21.

[39] *Seven Pillars of Wisdom* (Garden City, New York: Doubleday, Doran, and Co., 1935), pp. 39, 157.

[40] *Cambridge Ancient History* (New York: Macmillan, 1923–39), III (1925), 493.

[41] II Sam. 7:14; Hos. 11:1.

through whom God was mediated to the people."[42] The priestly representation of the community is illustrated by the judgment scene at which Joshua the high priest is acquitted.[43] Similar identification occurs with prominent laymen, such as Nehemiah: "I confess the sins of the children of Israel, which we have sinned against thee; yea, I and my father's house have sinned."[44] Similarly, the prophet owes his peculiar place as an intercessor with God,[45] to the fact that he temporarily becomes the nation, and makes its needs articulate. The profound sympathy of the prophet with the people whose doom he may have to foretell owes not a little to this corporate identity—"for the hurt of the daughter of my people am I hurt."[46] The principles of prophetic "symbolism" enabled a prophet to see the corporate significance of the individual. Thus it might be claimed that Hosea's relation to Gomer is not merely a private and personal affair made into a dramatic analogy; Gomer in both her sin and her anticipated repentance *is* the nation of which she is an actual sample and an epitomizing and representative unit. Later on, the Maccabean martyrs consciously identify themselves with the nation.[47] The principle of vicarious suffering which they exemplify and articulate is itself an application of social solidarity, in which it may be said to be latent.[48] In truth, the higher purpose of any group is always expressed by a minority within it, sometimes a minority of one. Yet the one or two remain the representatives of the group for the time being. We may compare the repeated transference of the theme of a symphony from

---

[42] "The Religious Aspects of Hebrew Kingship," *Zeitschrift für die alttestamentliche Wissenschaft*, Neue Folge, IX (1932, Heft 1), 37.
[43] Zech. 3:1–10.
[44] Neh. 1:6.
[45] E.g., Amos 7:2, 5.
[46] Jer. 8:21.
[47] II Macc. 7:38; IV Macc. 6:28–29, 17:21–22.
[48] S. A. Cook, *op. cit.*, p. 491.

one instrument or group of instruments to another; for the time being, each leads and represents the values of the whole orchestration. The most familiar of all examples of this representative value is seen in the thoroughly Hebraic contrast of Adam and Christ made by the Apostle Paul, which draws all its cogency from the conception of corporate personality: "as in Adam all die, so also in Christ shall all be made alive."[49]

(2) In the second place, our discussion of corporate personality bears on the much-debated question of the "I" of the Psalms and of the Servant of Yahweh. In regard to the Psalms, the collective interpretation which was urged by Smend in 1888,[50] and found wide acceptance in the early years of this century, seems to have given way to the individualistic view presented by Balla in 1912,[51] and largely employed by Gunkel in his commentary on the Psalms (1926).[52] On the other hand, Mowinckel[53] has emphasized what he calls "community mysticism," and applied it specially to the cult, remarking that "the conception of the community as a 'great ego' is genuinely Semitic—and genuinely primitive—, and makes itself felt particularly in the cult where the *communio sanctorum* emerges as a body

---

[49] I Cor. 15:22. T. W. Manson, in *The Teaching of Jesus* (Cambridge University Press, 1931), p. 227, has argued that the term "Son of man" in the Synoptic Gospels is itself a corporate conception, linked with that of the Old Testament.

[50] "Über das Ich der Psalmen," *Zeitschrift für die alttestamentliche Wissenschaft*, VIII (1888), 49–147.

[51] *Das Ich der Psalmen* ("Forschungen zur Religion und Literatur des Alten und Neuen Testaments," 16; Göttingen, 1912).

[52] Especially *Einleitung*, pp. 173–75 (1928). [*Einleitung in die Psalmen: Die Gattung der religiösen Lyrik Israels* ("Göttinger Handkommentar zum Alten Testament," Ergänzungsband; Göttingen: Vandenhoeck & Ruprecht, 1933). The commentary referred to above is *Die Psalmen, übersetzt und erklärt* (Göttinger Handkommentar zum Alten Testament," II Abteilung, Vol. II, 4th ed.; Göttingen: Vandenhoeck & Ruprecht, 1926).—EDITOR.]

[53] S. Mowinckel, *Psalmenstudien* (Oslo, 1921–24; reprinted, Amsterdam: P. Schippers, 1961), Buch I, pp. 164–65; cf. Buch V, pp. 36–38, Exkurs. [Cf. also Mowinckel's discussion in *The Psalms in Israel's Worship*, trans. D. R. Ap-Thomas (2 vols.; New York: Abingdon, 1962), especially pp. 42 ff.—EDITOR.]

and a soul." In this view he sees the element of truth in the argument of Smend, to which, as he says, Balla has not paid sufficient attention. The fact is that the conception of corporate personality for which we have argued largely removes the sharp antithesis between the collective and the individualistic views. Smend himself to some degree saw this, as when he says *so liegt dabei zunächst wenigstens keine rhetorische oder poetische Figur vor, die mit Bewusstsein gesucht würde. Es handelt sich hier vielmehr um einen ganz unwillkürlichen Ausdruck des Gemeingefühls.*[54] Balla does not meet this when he speaks[55] of *das regellose Hinundherschwanken zwischen einem Ich und Wir* as being without any *psychologischästhetische Begründung.* Nor is Gunkel any nearer the mark when he dismisses the collective view with contempt as *ein letzter Rest der früher allgemeingültigen allegorischen Deutung der heiligen Schrift* and says that it is psychologically impossible for the "I" of the poet to pass into the "I" of the community.[56] It is *not* psychologically impossible in view of the examples given, and a similar usage underlies the undeniable applications of Hebrew law. Moreover, the view we have presented is neither allegory nor personification, but a primitive category of thought which is very different from our own antithesis of the collective and the individual. The writer of a psalm is indeed always an individual and not a syndicate, and there is a sense in which it may be said that every psalm does represent an individual experience and outlook. It is also unnatural for a psalmist consciously to imagine himself as a community. But if the collective sense is so much a part of himself and of his outlook as it was with

---

[54] *Op. cit.,* p. 60. ["What we have then, in the first instance at least, is not a consciously contrived rhetorical or poetical figure. We are confronting, rather, a completely instinctive expression of communal feeling."—EDITOR.]

[55] *Op cit.,* pp. 133–34. ["... the irregular shifting back and forth between 'I' and 'we'" is without any "psychological-aesthetic foundation."—EDITOR.]

[56] *Einleitung in die Psalmen, op. cit.,* p. 175. ["... a final vestige of the allegorical sense previously applied everywhere to Holy Scripture ..."—EDITOR.]

the Israelite, then he can never wholly detach himself from the social horizon. The absence of our sharper distinctions and different starting-point will be seen in that fluidity of movement which has been emphasized; in Psalm 44, for example, there are no less than six transitions from the singular to the plural or from the plural to the singular. This is the poetic equivalent of many prose passages, such as the speech of Israel to Edom,[57] "We will go up by the high way: and if we drink of thy water, I and my cattle, then will I give the price thereof." How is this different from Psalm 44:6–7 [Eng. trans., 5–6]: "Through thy name will we tread them under that rise up against us. For I will not trust in my bow"? To explain this transition as Balla does[58] by reference to a supposed leader suddenly thinking of himself, is most unnatural, whereas the fluid conception of corporate personality at once supplies an adequate explanation, based, as Mowinckel rightly says,[59] "not on the external fact of representation through a single person, but on primitive psychology."

All that has been said about the "I" of the Psalms of course applies to the even more keenly debated question as to the identity of "the Servant of Yahweh" in Deutero-Isaiah. The great variety[60] of views which have been maintained by eminent scholars, and not less the oscillation[61] of the views of those scholars themselves, is provocative of thought.

---

[57] Num. 20:19, on which see G. Buchanan Gray, *Numbers (International Critical Commentary;* New York: Scribner's, 1903), pp. 265–66: he points out "that the characteristic and original names of nations are singulars—Moab, Edom, Israel, Midian, Jerahme'el."

[58] *Op. cit.,* pp. 108–9.

[59] *Psalmenstudien, op. cit.,* Buch V, p. 37.

[60] Conveniently tabulated by P. Volz, *Jesaia II übersetzt und erklärt* ("Kommentar zum Alten Testament," IX, 2; Leipzig: A. Deichertsche Verlagsbuchhandlung, 1932), p. 167. The identifications with outstanding individuals almost parallel Ben Sirach's catalog of the famous men of Israel, or the roll call of the heroes of faith in Hebrews 11.

[61] E.g., Duhm, Sellin, Gunkel, and Mowinckel.

Does it not suggest that the central issue, that between a collective and an individualistic interpretation, is being argued on an antithesis true to modern, but false to ancient modes of thought? To us there certainly seem to be data for both views in the "Songs," even apart from their contexts. But we have seen that the Hebrew conception of corporate personality can reconcile both, and pass without explanation or explicit indication from one to the other, in a fluidity of transition which seems to us unnatural. In the light of this conception the Servant can be both the prophet himself as representative of the nation, and the nation whose proper mission is actually being fulfilled only by the prophet and that group of followers who may share his views. To say this is not to take refuge in a vague and ambiguous formula, though the formula may be difficult enough to express and apply in translation and exegesis. Ancient literature never does fit exactly into our categories.

Let us rapidly review the four "Songs" from this standpoint. In the first (Isa. 42:1-4) the mission of the Servant is to the "nations" (gōyim) of the earth, and such an international mission suggests national activity by the people Yahweh has chosen. Even if none yet shared this outlook with the prophet, his consciousness of it is instinctively nationalistic. He conceives Israel as meekly accepting its national suffering, and active through its missionary propaganda. The individualizing features do not go beyond those of the normal Hebrew imagination, e.g., as applied elsewhere to Babylon (47:1-3), or Zion (54:1-2).

In the second Song (49:1-6), the prophet-Servant is burdened with the sense of the blindness and deafness of the actual Israel (42:19), and says, "I have toiled in vain"; but he is encouraged by the promise of a wider mission than that of converting his own nation—that world-mission which requires indeed a converted nation for its fulfillment. This is just the sort of paradox in which religion delights; a man is strengthened for a smaller task by being shown a larger one. The movement of thought in vv. 5 and 6 is from the smaller to the larger mission of the Servant;[62] the prophet's consciousness, and with it his conception of the Servant's mission and the connotation of the name, expand through the conversion of his fellow Israelites to the fulfillment of the national mission. The prophet is conscious of no contrast during that expansion. He *is* Israel created to be the Servant; he is Israel, though working alone to make Israel what she ought to be; he is Israel finally become a light of nations to the end of the earth. This seems to be better described as "realism" than as a contrast of the "ideal" collective personality and the "real" individual.[63] The English term "ideal" is a dangerous one to use of a people so realistic in their thinking as Israel. The scope of actuality expands or contrasts in the way suggested, but never passes beyond what imagination actualizes as "real," whether in the one or the many. In the third Song (50:4–9), the Servant is strengthened against suffering by fellowship with God, whether the opposition encountered be Jewish or Gentile. Because of divine help he is confident that his mission will be fulfilled. Here too the experience of God is individual, whilst the mission for God is collective; Hebrew thought is content to bring them into juxtaposition, because corporate personality could reconcile both. In the fourth Song (52:13—53:12), it is Israel as a whole—now restored to its former home and so vindicated—on which the many na-

---

[62] It is more natural to take *l^{e}shōbhēbh* ["to bring back"], etc. as referring to the *'ebhedh* ["Servant"] and not as a gerundial expression of Yahweh's purpose in *'āmar* [the Lord "says"]; but this does not really affect the above argument.

[63] Cf. Eissfeldt, *Der Gottesknecht bei Deuterojesaja (Jes. 40–55) im Lichte der israelitischen Anschauung von Gemeinschaft und Individuum* (Halle, 1933), p. 25; Eng. trans., "The Ebed-Jahwe in Isaiah xl.–lv. in the Light of the Israelite Conceptions of the Community and the Individual, the Ideal and the Real," *The Expository Times*, XLIV (1933), 261–68. I am in general agreement with his argument, which makes a use of corporate personality similar to that outlined above, but independently of my book *The Cross of the Servant* (London: SCM, 1926), in which it was presented.

tions gaze in wonder.[64] The past sufferings of the exile are now seen in a new light; they were thought to be deserved penalty, but they are really vicarious suffering for the nations themselves in a larger solidarity; they have become, in fact, a sacrificial offering *('āshām)* through which the nations can approach Yahweh.[65] This has come about because the prophet's spirit has become that of the nation and because Yahweh has vindicated the faith of his Servant by a national resurrection from the grave of exile. The double *motif,* i.e., the national mission and the individual vocation, is thus carried through to the end, and it is made possible for Hebrew thought by the reconciling principle of corporate personality.

(3) We have seen how the principle works in the representation of the group by the individual, and in the expansion of the individual consciousness to that of the group; we may now glance at its working within the group in the relation of its members to one another. This is the field of Hebrew morality, limited[66] and yet intensified by the sense of corporate personality. As S. A. Cook says, "Ethical ideas are at least implicit in the group-idea, for the social group protected its poor and weak members—provided the group-sentiment was strong."[67] It is interesting to compare Hebrew ethics with those of the Greeks, more individualized because springing from the idea of an artificial state, and based on the relation of the individual to social traditions and political order.[68] Greek ethics was concerned with life as a whole—"the harmonious adjustment of the ele-

---

[64] Cf. Ps. 126:2 for a similar Gentile attitude.

[65] The only textual difficulty is *'ammū* in 53:8, which must be read as *'ammīm* (cf. Lam. 3:14, where there is good support from manuscripts and the Syriac for correcting the same error).

[66] Cf. G. Buchanan Gray, *The Divine Discipline of Israel* (London: A. and C. Black, 1900), p. 46.

[67] *Op. cit.,* p. 439.

[68] Cf. John Dewey and J. H. Tufts, *Ethics* (New York: Henry Holt, 1908), p. 111.

ments in man's nature—material and spiritual, individual and social,"[69] whereas the cruder and narrower outlook of the Hebrews derived from its nomadic period. T. H. Robinson has well said of Israel, "She brought with her from the nomad stage a conception of common brotherhood which she was the first to apply to the conditions of a highly organized settled community . . . to every other ancient monarch the subject was a slave, to the Israelite king he was a brother."[70] When we look back to those nomadic conditions, as for example they are depicted in Doughty's *Arabia Deserta*, we see at once the nomadic strain in the classical epitome of prophetic morality—"to do justice and to love mercy."[71] Doughty says, "in the opinion of the next governed countries, the Arabs of the wilderness are the justest of mortals" and "In the hospitality of the Arabs is kinship and assurance, in their insecure countries. This is the piety of the Arab life, this is the sanctity of the Arabian religion, where we may not look for other."[72] In close relation to this is the law of blood-feud, which is the true measure of effective kinship.[73] If we take such cross sections of the development of Hebrew morality as are afforded, say, by the Book of the Covenant, the Law of Holiness (Lev. 19) and Job's *apologia pro vita sua* (chap. 31), it is easy to see the presence of both justice and mercy throughout, and their development within the group. If *mishpāt* stands for the original element of tribal custom, *hesed* represents that mingling of duty and love which springs directly from

---

[69] J. H. Muirhead, "Ethics," in *Encyclopaedia of Religion and Ethics*, ed. James Hastings (Edinburgh: T. and T. Clark, and New York: Scribner's. 1908–27), V (1912), 422.

[70] *Palestine in General History* (Schweich Lectures for 1926; Oxford University Press, 1929), pp. 41 and 44.

[71] Mic. 6:8.

[72] C. M. Doughty, *Travels in Arabia Deserta* (Cambridge University Press, 1888), I, 249; II, 152.

[73] W. Robertson Smith, *Kinship and Marriage in Early Arabia, op. cit.*, p. 22.

the conception of common ties, and expands to include and regulate the conception of Yahweh's relation to Israel, so uniting morality and religion in the most characteristic feature of all Israel's development. We do not exaggerate when we say that Hebrew morality, and consequently Christian morality, are what they are because they sprang up within a society dominated by the principle of corporate personality.

If the argument of this paper is sound, its theme is of considerable importance for the interpretation of the Old Testament, and deserves more attention than it has received. Again and again, we have to put ourselves back to a view of things very different from our own. A good and interesting example of this may be borrowed from Wolf's account[74] of Egyptian art. Egyptian wall-paintings show the absence of all perspective and a stereotyped rectangular view of the subject. This, he argues, is the unconscious result of that community-emphasis of which Egypt is so striking an example. On the other hand, perspective drawing in the full sense did not come in till our own Renaissance times, and was itself connected with the rise of modern individualism, since perspective always implies a particular and individualized point of view. Thus the ancient drawings in the flat would be something like the popular ballad or myth, a product of the corporate personality of Egypt, a view of things as all might see them. The illustration is a useful one to remember, for it may remind us always to get back from our own modern standpoint to that more corporate and social view of things which is so striking a feature of the Old Testament.

[74] *Op. cit.,* pp. 7–16. This brief study is of great interest.

The Group and the
Individual in Israel

At the outset of any historical survey of the relations of
society and the individual, and particularly of those within
Israel, there are three general considerations which deserve
to be mentioned. The first is that there can never be any
ultimate and exclusive antithesis of the two. The individual
could not come into existence at all without some form of
society, and depends upon it for his growth and development. The society finds articulate expression only through
the individuals who constitute it. Human personality is in
itself as truly social as individual. Differences of emphasis
will be felt in different periods, and it seems generally true
that a predominant consciousness of the group pre-
cedes the fuller discovery of the individual. But it would
be wrong to suppose that in the earlier period of Israel's
history, for example, there was little or no consciousness
of the individual; the point is rather that the individual
was then *more* conscious of being one of the group. It
would be equally wrong to suppose that, in the later
period, the greater sense of individuality altogether

excluded the consciousness of membership in a corporate unity. In all the generations, past and present, the systole and the diastole of both individuality and sociality are heard in the heartbeats of humanity.

The second point is that there was much more fluidity in the ancient conception of both the group and the individual, so that one could merge into the other much more easily than our modern categories allow. Thus the society could find realistic incorporation in an individual who represented it, such as the king or priest, and the individual instinctively enlarged his own consciousness so as to speak confidently in the name of the whole group, as does the prophet and the psalmist in Israel.

The third point is that in the interpretation of the contemporary social order, the individual tends to project his own idea of himself. The subjectivity which we see in Rousseau's *Confessions* passed into the individualism of his *Social Contract* and the theories which so influenced the French Revolution. Indeed, it often seems that it is the psychology of an age which shapes its sociology. Thus Plato explicitly makes the ideal state parallel in its elements with those of the individual person: "In each of us there are the same principles and habits which there are in the State,"[1] i.e., the rational, the spirited, and the appetitive. The Hebrew psychology, on the other hand, started not with an indwelling soul, but with an animated body, each of its physical members having psychical and ethical qualities. Personality was a "United States" rather than an empire. In correspondence with this psychology the Hebrew society (in spite of its monarchical government during part of its history) is of essentially democratic character, very conscious that each of its members has rights of his own.

With these considerations in mind, we shall review: (1)

---

[1] *Republic*, iv. 435, Jowett's translation.

The primary place of the Group in Israel; (2) The emergence of the Individual through the prophetic consciousness; (3) The Jewish and the Christian Synthesis of this individualism into new group-unities.

1

The Primary Place of the Group

The essentially democratic character of Hebrew society goes back to, and derives from, its nomadic period. The Book of Deuteronomy (chap. 26) contains a liturgy of thanksgiving, in which the Israelite looks back across the basket of firstfruits he is presenting to Yahweh and humbly acknowledges that "A wandering Aramean was my father" [Deut. 26:5]. There are links with that nomadic past in the familiar stories of the patriarchs and of the wanderings after the Exodus from Egypt; and to that idealized past the great prophets return to gain a reproachful background for the sorry present. But the actual story of that past must have been much simpler and cruder than is represented in the stories and traditions; its real nature may be seen from such a book as Doughty's *Arabia Deserta,* which describes the little changed Bedouins of the nineteenth century.[2]

The nomadic clan must have been large enough to defend itself, and on occasion to attack other groups, yet not so large as to outrun the water supply at the oases in its range of journeyings. Its tie was one of blood, real or assumed, except for the protected "foreigners" who were of necessity attached to it—since the desert is no home for the isolated individual. The protective principle of the clan was that of blood-revenge, by which each member of the group was pledged to exact vengeance, for a wrong done to his

[2] C. M. Doughty, *Travels in Arabia Deserta* (Cambridge University Press, 1888).

fellow, from members of the group to which the offending man belonged. It is a nomad's boast of blood-revenge that is preserved for us in "The Song of Lamech" (Gen. 4:23–24):

> Hear my voice, O wives of Lamech,
>   listen to my word;
> A man do I slay for my bruise,
>   and a child for my stripe.
> For seven times shall Cain be avenged,
> But Lamech seventy times and seven.

From such unrestricted vendetta which magnifies the offence and multiplies its victims from the hostile clan, it is a real advance in morality to reach the *lex talionis* of Israel's first code of law in Canaan (Exod. 21:24–25), viz., "wound for wound, stripe for stripe," instead of many wounds or stripes for one.

The nomad clan continued to be the effective group unit even after the settlement of the Israelites in Canaan: David is represented as asking Jonathan's permission to be away from court that he may attend the annual sacrifice of his clan at Bethlehem (I Sam. 20:6). Such a clan would contain a number of what *we* should call "families"; on the other hand, a group of clans tracing by genealogy a more distant blood-connection constituted in theory the "tribe." In theory, for the familiar "tribes of Israel," sprung from the twelve sons of Jacob, are a genealogical fiction. The actual grouping of Israelites into such larger units was due rather to geographical settlement, mixed marriages, conquest or assimilation of other groups, including the Canaanites themselves and groups of Israelites who probably settled in Canaan directly from the desert without sharing in the experiences of the Exodus.

If we would picture the normal group-life of the Israelites settled in Canaan, we must think primarily of a limited number of families gathered in a village or small town. The common sacrificial meal to which Samuel invited the youthful Saul had thirty guests (I Sam. 9:22); we may assume that these were the "elders," the heads of the families composing the village. The communal affairs would be in the hands of these elders, who met to discuss them "in the gate." Such a scene is well described for us in the Book of Ruth (chap. 4), when Boaz arranges to take over the rights and duties of the nearest kinsman of Naomi, in order that he may marry the widowed daughter-in-law of Naomi. Ten elders are chosen; the business is discussed; a symbolic action marks its decision, and the bystanders with the elders are called to witness it. The incident may be taken to illustrate not only the communal life of the village or town, but also the quite subordinate place of women in the social order. They were the property of their father or their husband who would naturally represent them and defend their interests; but widows and orphan boys or girls who had no relative to take their part "in the gate" were an easy prey for the oppressor. That is why we hear so many admonitions from lawmakers or prophets to defend and help these classes left without representative defenders. The same thing applies to "the stranger within thy gates," but we should note that this phrase refers to the resident foreigner who had become the "permanent guest" of the clan and to some extent shared its rights and duties. (A quite different word describes the wholly detached foreigner, who occupied a very different position as an "unnaturalized alien.")[3]

The slave occupied a much better position than the word suggests to modern ears. As his master's property, he was in a more dependent condition than that of the protected "strangers"; on the other hand, the more intimate relations of the slave to a particular family gave him a more assured

---

[3] ["Stranger within thy gates," "sojourner" (R.S.V.), as at Exod. 20:10, is in Hebrew *gēr;* for the foreigner or "unnaturalized alien" a different word, *zār,* is used (R.S.V., "outsider," as at Exod. 29:33), or *nokrī,* "foreigner," as at Gen. 31:15.—EDITOR.]

position and evoked particular interests on his behalf. A foreign slave could be held for life, but the servitude of a Hebrew slave was limited to six years, and the earliest code of Hebrew law contemplates his saying at the end of that period, "I love my master, my wife, and my children; I will not go out free" (Exod. 21:5). Such a slave might become a trusted friend, like him whom Abraham sent to his kinsfolk in Aram to choose a wife for Isaac.

We have been thinking so far of the smaller local group, with which the individual stood in closest relation. Beyond this was the tribal association of such clans, usually occupying a common geographical area, which had its own particular interests. But, beyond this again, was the largest and most important unity, that of Israel. However mixed in blood its original elements were, and however strong the disintegrating influences of a country which has well been called "a land of tribes" rather than the land of a united nation, the national unity became a most important fact for the history of Israel. It is characteristic of the genius and eventual contribution of Israel that this national unity was from the outset based on religion. It has already been suggested that not all the later "Israelites" went down to Egypt and returned to invade Canaan, but that some of them had long since settled there. Be this as it may, it was the Josephites (as we may call the Egyptian contingent) who were destined to form the nucleus of the future nation. They were welded into an aggressive unity sufficient to force their way into parts of Canaan by their faith in Yahweh as their war-god. That which made Him different from the war-gods of other similar Semitic groups was their wonderful escape from the Egyptians under His leadership and the light which this escape threw on His nature and purpose. He was believed to have freely chosen this particular group for Himself and to require from it a fidelity doubtless crude and limited enough in detail, but moral in spirit. Yahweh was forever "the out-of-Egypt bringing God" (as a German might phrase it); Israel was the chosen people, linked to Him by no quasi-physical tie such as that of a nature-God, but by a moral act. It was this relation which (under changing forms and details of expression) underlay the covenant of Yahweh with His people. The relation of moral obligation as well as of feeling has a special name (*ḥesed*) in Hebrew, which is inadequately translated as "loving-kindness." It means much the same as *agápē* in the New Testament. Observe that the covenant is with the nation, not with the individual Israelites except as members or representatives of the nation. Throughout the whole period of the Old Testament, this covenant with the "corporate personality" of Israel (as we may call it) remains the all-inclusive fact and factor, whatever the increase in the consciousness of individuality.

Two examples will make this conception clearer. They may be taken from two of the greatest poems of the Old Testament literature. One of them, the Song of Deborah [Judg. 5], is our earliest document for the history of Israel. The other, the Song of the Servant [Isa. 42:1–4, 49:1–6, 50:4–9, and 52:13—53:12], closes the era of the great prophets, and forms the culminating glory of Old Testament religion. In both there is the unitary conception of the corporate personality of Israel.

In the Song of Deborah we hear of the danger in which the scattered groups of Israel stood from the pressure of the Canaanites. The Israelites are not simply scattered geographically; they are disunited in interest. Judah, Simeon, and Levi are not mentioned, probably because they had no tribal existence at this time, i.e., a generation or two after the first entrance of the Josephites into Canaan. The Song praises those who came to the help of Yahweh, viz., Issachar, Zebulun, Naphtali, Machir-Manasseh, Ephraim, and Benjamin. It blames severely those who stood aloof, viz., Reuben, Gilead-Gad, Dan, and Asher. (These all dwelt at a greater distance from the plain where the battle was fought, which meant that their immediate interests were not so much at stake.) Perhaps this was the first great occasion of common action in Canaan, and the significant thing for us is that the unity is defined simply as a common loyalty to Yahweh, who came from his mountain home in the south as the storm-god to help his people Israel win their battle through storm and flood:

> The stars in their courses fought against Sisera,
> The river Kishon swept them away.
>> (Judges 5:20–21).

Over against this battle-song of the earliest days, we may set the Songs of the Servant of the Lord, particularly that of Isaiah 53. It represents Israel in her corporate personality, Israel going down to national death in exile, yet to be divinely raised in a national restoration to her former home. The prophet hears the future confession of the nations of the earth, when they behold that resurrection and see how they have misjudged this people. That which seemed divine penalty for sin is now seen as vicarious suffering for the nations, a sacrificial offering through which *they* may approach the God of Israel. Between the militant passion of the Song of Deborah and the sacrificial passion of the Song of the Servant, a whole world of religious development lies; but it is throughout the group conception of Israel that is primary. In both Songs, the individual has, of course, his place, whether Deborah and Barak and Jael, or the unknown prophet of the exile who is calling for a religious consciousness in all Israelites like his own. But in both we see that it is the group which occupies the foreground of thought and feeling, since Yahweh is always the covenanted God of *Israel*.

2

The Emergence of the Individual
through the Prophetic Consciousness

It was characteristic that the national unity of Israel should have been created and sustained by its religion. It was equally characteristic that the fuller sense of individuality should be a product of the prophetic consciousness. This fuller sense came through the religious experience of men who believed that they stood in an individual relation both to God and the nation. They were the eyes of the people toward God and the mouth of God toward the people (Isa. 29:10, Jer. 15:19). From their individual call onward, their experience and their message alike isolated them in greater or less degree; thus the prophet Jeremiah cries to God, "I sat not in the assembly of them that make merry, nor rejoiced: I sat alone because of thy hand" (15:17). No man can be forced into such isolation from the natural fellowships of life without one of two things happening. Either he will become sullen and embittered, or else he will find consolation and compensation in a deeper sense of God. The God of Israel was always conceived as a Person, and there is no surer way of deepening our own personality than fellowship with a greater one. In discovering what the greater personality is, we discover our own. The process by which the prophet came to reflect the thought and feeling of God exalted him into a new consciousness of individual worth to God. This initial factor made the prophets pioneers of a richer sense of individual personality and able to leave behind them a legacy which has become part of the spiritual inheritance of the world.

But the initial factor, their own relation to God, was reinforced by the very demands they made of Israel in the name of God. "Cease to do evil, learn to do well; seek justice, make the violent keep straight; give judgment for the orphan, support the cause of the widow" (Isa. 1:16–17). Their message was to the nation, but they asked justice and mercy from the individual Israelite toward his neighbor as the true and essential fulfillment of God's desires, without which the ritual of worship became a mockery. This social ethic was the direct development of the old nomadic clan spirit, purified and enlightened, and raised to the level of a religious offering to God. The corporate personality of Israel could not stand in a right relation to God unless it approached Him in this unity of internal and individual fellowship. Such a demand, so conceived, even when presented to the nation, became inevitably a demand for an *individual* response to it. Moreover, it became increasingly a demand for something more than the *external* reformation of conduct. Hosea saw that what was wrong with Israel was its inner spirit of infidelity (4:12, 5:4). The only fulfillment of God's law was love. The book of Deuteronomy, largely influenced by Hosea's teaching, proclaimed, "Thou shalt love Yahweh thy God" (6:5), and justified the paradox of a law to love by presenting Yahweh as a lovable, because a redeeming, God (6:21 ff.). Jeremiah, saying, "Thou art near in their mouth and far from their affections" (12:2), is contrasting the common shout of praise with the individual motive to thanksgiving. This new emphasis on motive went far to individualize the relation of the Israelite to Yahweh.

But the religious experience of the prophets went farther still in this process of individualization. They were themselves sustained in their mission by the personal fellowship of God, the experience of which one of them wrote, "morning by morning He wakeneth mine ear to hear as a disciple" (Isa. 50:4). Some of them came to see that they were making a demand on the individual Israelites which could be fulfilled only by divine aid, God's acts of individualizing grace. So we have the promise of a "new covenant" through Jeremiah, which should be individualized and internalized, in contrast with all previous covenants which had been national and expressed in external forms: "I will put my law in their inward parts, and in their heart will I write it" (31:31 ff.). It is still a covenant "with the house of Israel," but it is accomplished through a new and more searching relation of God to each member of that house. So also with the promise of grace through Jeremiah's younger contemporary, Ezekiel (36:26–27): "A new heart will I give you, and a new spirit will I put within you; and I will take away the stony heart out of your flesh, and I will give you a heart of flesh. And I will put my spirit within you, and cause you to walk in my statutes."

This new individualization of the relation of Israel to God is confirmed by the fact that Ezekiel (chap. 18) proclaims individual moral responsibility in sharper terms than anyone before him. "The soul that sinneth, *it* shall die"—not others also, as the older conception of corporate personality had demanded from Achan's family (Josh. 7:24 ff.).

If we think of the prophets of Israel as a spiritual aristocracy, then we may say that what they hoped for was a democratization of their own relation to God, when all the Lord's people would be prophets (Num. 11:29), and God would pour out his spirit upon all flesh (Joel 2:28). Indeed, we may say in general of the "great men" of Israel, those outstanding personalities which are so prominent in her history, that they are what they are precisely in this way. Their human personality is again and again shown to be achieved as a response to the call and influence of divine personality. It might well be argued, even on purely philosophical grounds, that no profounder interpretation of human personality could ever be given.

3

The Syntheses Made by Judaism and Christianity

From this religious individualism *within* the still retained group-consciousness there came in course of time a twofold synthesis, viz., that of Judaism and that of Christianity. We may draw a homely illustration from the lump of coal. Behind the coal seam there lies the long perspective of primeval forests and luxuriant vegetation which have lived and died to create it. The coal itself will yield both gas and coke, each product bringing its own chain of industrial developments. So we may think of the religion of Israel ultimately depositing the literature of the Old Testament, which has become the source of two great religions, viz., Judaism and Christianity, each with its far-reaching influence on the history of the world.

The new synthesis of individual Israelites which we call Judaism becomes visible only after the exile and the return of some of the exiles. But the synthesis of those individuals who were to shape a new future really began with such a group as the disciples who gathered round Isaiah (Isa. 8:16). Such fellowship is seen again and again, notably in the pious circles from which many of the psalms came, and in the group of which we hear in the book of Malachi: "Then they that feared the Lord spake one with another: and the Lord hearkened and heard, and a book of remembrance was written before him, for them that feared the Lord and that thought upon his name" (3:16). We have their spiritual descendants in the Hasidim, those enthusiasts for the Jewish Law who supported Judas Maccabeus (I Macc. 2:42) so long as he was fighting for religious liberty (7:13). From these again came the Pharisees, those religious leaders of the ordinary people who were destined to shape its religious future and to remain supreme as the rabbis of the Mishnah and Talmud, after the Jewish War had eliminated their chief rivals, the Sadducees. It is important to realize that this was a new synthesis and not merely the postexilic continuation of preexilic Israel. Those who did return from exile were the chosen few who had learned from the prophets that repentance was fundamental in any right relation to God. The ritual of the Temple, and later, the legalism of the Torah might limit or modify the spirituality of this individual relation to God but by no means destroyed it. Further, we find that the most important and influential change of doctrine, the belief in a real life beyond death, which was absent from the religion of Israel and was developed in Judaism, is itself necessarily a belief concerning the individual. Not all Gentiles would be excluded from, and not all Jews would be admitted to, that future life. The nation remained—and remains still for the Jew—as a fact and as a privilege, an individual opportunity, not a guarantee, of blessedness and resurrection from the dead.

The Christian synthesis was affiliated to the same line of development of the religious group within the national group, but it emphasized the prophetic and apocalyptic rather than the legalistic and moralistic features of that development, whilst sharing in the Jewish hope of life beyond death. The new fact, the crystallizing center for Judaism, had been the Torah, the Law ascribed to Moses, both written (the Pentateuch) and unwritten ("the tradition of the elders," Mark 7:3). The present arrangement of the Old Testament literature reflects the later belief of Judaism, which turned the literary result of the whole development into a revelation given to Moses on Sinai. In that sense the Old Testament is a Jewish book, whereas the Christian arrangement might have been a different one (had change then been possible), giving primacy to the prophets. The new fact for Christianity was not a Book, but a Person. Jesus came as the Jewish Prophet-Messiah, but completely transformed the title by preferring the transcendent and apocalyptic to the political and nationalistic idea, and blending with it the conception of the suffering Servant of the Lord. Around him a new group formed, that of his immediate disciples, a new Israel of God.

St. Paul has shown us this group at a further stage of its development, using the metaphor of the body of Christ. Here we see the new synthesis in clearest form, especially if we interpret the metaphor, as we should, by Hebrew and not by Greek psychology. In the Hebrew conception, the body, not the soul, is the essential personality; the body is indeed animated by the soul, in each of its members, but then each of these, by a sort of diffused consciousness, shares in the psychical and ethical, as well as in the physical, life of the body. Thus St. Paul (I Cor. 12:12 ff.) is led to conceive those who are spiritually gathered round Christ by faith in him as members of his body. They vary in function and rank, but they are made one by the unity of the body, animated as it is by the one Spirit of the Lord. This is the most explicit utterance of the Bible concerning the relation of the group and the individual. It implies a new kind of individual, but one who, like the true Israelite of old, could never be divorced from his social relationship.

Other lecturers in this series[4] have reminded us that the relation of the group to the individual is a present-day issue, and have indicated the bearing of their study of the past upon the present. What might be learned from our review of the emergence of the individual in Israel? First, that all progress comes through individual initiative and through the action of a minority. Israel's history has contributed so

---

[4] [Undergraduate lectures at Oxford in 1936 on "The Individual in East and West"; see Introduction to the First Edition, p. 22.—EDITOR.]

greatly to religion partly because it was the history of a community in which there was so much scope and freedom for the individual life. This was in no small degree due to the democratic traditions of the desert, which persisted long in Canaan. T. E. Lawrence says truly of the Semitic races, "They were a people of spasms, of upheavals, of ideas, the race of the individual genius."[5] "The Semites' idea of nationality was the independence of clans and villages."[6] So the history of Israel is largely the story of its great individuals, pioneers in the discovery of religious truth—Moses, Elijah, Amos, Hosea, Isaiah, Jeremiah, and Deutero-Isaiah. Freedom for individual utterance remains the essential condition of national progress, as our own Milton so vigorously pleaded in his *Areopagitica*.

In the second place, the progress made by Israel to a larger truth was conditioned by a lively faith in the spiritual and unseen world, for which its great individuals became the spokesmen. Without such loyalty to something greater and more lasting than the passing fashions of thought in a single generation, there can be no lasting gain, even if there is gain at all. Graham Wallas, in his classical book, *The Great Society*, after speaking of the value and necessity of individual initiative, rightly goes on to say, "Napoleon on the Imperial throne, the financial genius when he has overcome his rivals, the leader of young opinion when his books are read and his plays acted in twenty languages, may create nothing but confusion and weakness unless his power is related to some greater purpose, in whose service is liberty."[7] Mere civilization and culture without religion become as perilous as did the culture of Canaan to Israel's historic purpose and destiny. In fact, there is some truth in

---

[5] *Seven Pillars of Wisdom* (Garden City, New York: Doubleday, Doran, and Co., 1935), p. 39.

[6] *Ibid.*, p. 100.

[7] *The Great Society: a Psychological Analysis* (New York: Macmillan, 1914), p. 83.

the pessimistic words of a Russian thinker, Rostovtzeff: "Is not every civilization bound to decay as soon as it begins to penetrate the masses?"[8] Democracy is too often like the loudspeaker which coarsens the voice and may make it unrecognizable. Popularization, even of religious truth, means some compromise of its truthfulness. There is always need of the individual, who endures in the strength of the vision he has seen, and endures in the often ungrateful task of urging the valley crowd to climb the heights with him. It is religion alone, in one form or another, which can make —not the world safe for democracy, but democracy safe for the world.

[8] As quoted in J. L. and B. Hammond, *The Bleak Age* ("Swan Library," 26; New York: Longmans, 1934), p. vi.

For Further Reading

By H. Wheeler Robinson

Deuteronomy and Joshua, Vol. IV in "The Century Bible," ed. W. F. ADENEY. Edinburgh: T. C. & E. C. Jack, 1907.

"Hebrew Psychology in Relation to Pauline Anthropology," in *Mansfield College Essays Presented to the Reverend Andrew Martin Fairbairn, D.D. on the occasion of his Seventieth Birthday, November 4, 1908.* London: Hodder and Stoughton, 1909. Pp. 265–86.

"Baptist Principles before the rise of Baptist Churches," in *The Baptists of Yorkshire* (1911), pp. 3–50. Reprinted as *Baptist Principles* ("Christian Education Manuals"). London: Kingsgate, 1925; third ed., 1938. Paperback ed., Greenwood, S. C.: Attic, 1955, German trans., 1931; Danish trans., 1939.

The Christian Doctrine of Man. Edinburgh: T. & T. Clark, 1911. Second ed., 1913; third ed., 1926.

The Religious Ideas of the Old Testament ("Studies in Theology," 24). London: Duckworth, 1913. Second ed., rev. by L. H. BROCKINGTON; London: Duckworth, and Naperville: Allenson, 1956.

The Cross of Job. London: SCM, 1916. Second rev. ed., "Religion and Life Books," 1938.

The Cross of Jeremiah. London: SCM, 1925.

The Cross of the Servant. London: SCM, 1926.

The Cross in the Old Testament. London: SCM, 1955, and Philadelphia: Westminster, 1956. Reprints *The Cross of Job* (1916), pp. 9–54; *The Cross of the Servant* (1926), pp. 55–114; and *The Cross of Jeremiah* (1925), pp. 115–92, though the original appendices and bibliographies are omitted.

"Hebrew Psychology," in *The People and the Book,* ed. A. S. PEAKE. Oxford University Press, 1925. Pp. 353–82.

The Life and Faith of the Baptists ("The Faiths" series). London: Methuen, 1927, and Greenwood, S. C.: Attic, 1946.

The Christian Experience of the Holy Spirit ("The Library of Constructive Theology"). London: Nisbet, and New York: Harper, 1928. Seventh ed., 1940.

The Veil of God ("The New Library of Devotion"). London: Nisbet, 1936.

"The Old Testament Background," in *Christian Worship: Studies in its History and Meaning,* ed. N. MICKLEM. Oxford University Press, 1936. Pp. 19–34.

"The Christian Doctrine of Redemption," in *The Christian Faith,* ed. W. R. MATTHEWS. London: Eyre & Spottiswoode, 1936. Pp. 209–31.

The Old Testament: its Making and Meaning. University of London Press, and Nashville: Cokesbury, 1937.

The History of Israel: its Facts and Factors ("Studies in Theology," 42). London: Duckworth, 1938. Second rev. ed., paperback, 1963.

Record and Revelation: Essays on the Old Testament by Members of the Society for Old Testament Study, ed. H. WHEELER ROBINSON. Oxford: Clarendon, 1938. Includes Robinson's essay, "The Theology of the Old Testament (The Philosophy of Revelation and The Characteristic Doctrines)," pp. 303–48.

"Law and Religion in Israel," in *Judaism and Christianity,* ed. E. I. J. ROSENTHAL. London: Sheldon, and New York: Macmillan, 1937–38. Vol. III (1938), pp. 45–66.

Suffering, Human and Divine ("Great Issues of Life" series). London: SCM, and New York: Macmillan, 1939.

"The Religion of Israel," in *A Companion to the Bible,* ed. T. W. MANSON. Edinburgh: T. & T. Clark, 1939. Pp. 287–331.

The Bible in its Ancient and English Versions, ed. H. WHEELER ROBINSON. Oxford: Clarendon, 1940. Includes two essays by Robinson, "The Hebrew Bible," pp. 1–38, and "The Bible as the Word of God," pp. 275–302.

Redemption and Revelation in the Actuality of History ("The Library of Constructive Theology"). London: Nisbet, 1942.

Inspiration and Revelation in the Old Testament. Oxford: Clarendon, 1946. ("Speaker's Lectures" at Oxford, 1942–45, presenting a prolegomena for Robinson's proposed Old Testament theology. Now available in an Oxford University Press paperback.)

The Cross of Hosea, ed. E. A. PAYNE. Philadelphia: Westminster, 1949. (See next title.)

Two Hebrew Prophets: Studies in Hosea and Ezekiel, ed. E. A. PAYNE. London: Lutterworth, 1959, and Naperville: Allenson, 1962. (Lectures from 1935 and 1943 respectively; those on Hosea were published separately in the United States in 1949, as noted above.)

About H. Wheeler Robinson

PAYNE, ERNEST A. *Henry Wheeler Robinson, Scholar, Teacher, Principal: A Memoir.* London: Nisbet, 1946. In addition to the biographical memoir (pp. 9–109), a selected bibliography, and portrait of Robinson, seven of his previously unpublished lectures are included.

————. *Studies in History and Religion Presented to Dr. H. Wheeler Robinson, M.A., on his seventieth birthday.* London: Lutterworth, 1942. A full portrait and a more detailed bibliography are included; the bibliography lists articles for commentaries, dictionaries, and encyclopedias, but by no means all his articles for popular journals nor his book reviews.

About Corporate Personality and Related Topics

For Robinson's later remarks, see especially *Record and Revelation,* pp. 332 f.; *Redemption and Revelation,* pp. 149 f., 246, 258–62, 281 f., 287–89; and *Inspiration and Revelation,* pp. 70 f., 81–85, 169 f., and 264.

JOHNSON, AUBREY R. *The One and the Many in the Israelite Conception of God.* Cardiff: University of Wales Press, 1942; ²1961. Especially pp. 1–22.

————. *The Vitality of the Individual in the Thought of Ancient Israel.* Cardiff: University of Wales Press, 1949. Pp. 83, n. 2, and 102, n. 2. Johnson disputes Wheeler Robinson's view about "diffusion of consciousness" (whereby limbs or organs of the body seem to function independently) and explains such Old Testament passages as synecdoche.

LATTEY, C. "Vicarious Solidarity in the Old Testament," *Vetus Testamentum,* 1 (1951), 267–74.

JACOB, EDMOND. *Theology of the Old Testament.* Translated by ARTHUR W. HEATHCOTE and PHILIP J. ALLCOCK. London: Hodder and Stoughton, and New York: Harper, 1958. Pp. 153–56.

MENDENHALL, G. E. "The Relation of the Individual to Political Society in Ancient Israel," in *Biblical Studies in Memory of H. C. Alleman,* ed. J. M. Myers. Locust Valley, New York: J. J. Augustin Publisher, 1960. Pp. 89–108.

PORTER, J. R. "Legal Aspects of Corporate Personality," *Vetus Testamentum,* 15 (1965), 361–80.

ROGERSON, J. W. "The Hebrew Conception of Corporate Personality: A Reconsideration," *Journal of Theological Studies,* 21 (1970), 1–16.

ROGERSON, J. W. *Anthropology and the Old Testament.* Oxford: Basil Blackwell, 1978, and Atlanta: John Knox, 1979.

THE SERVANT

NORTH, CHRISTOPHER R. *The Suffering Servant in Deutero-Isaiah: An Historical and Critical Study.* Oxford University Press, 1948; [2]1956. Pp. 3 f., 103–16, 202–7; cf. p. 210, n. 2.

——. "Servant of the Lord, The," in *The Interpreter's Dictionary of the Bible.* New York: Abingdon, 1962. Vol. IV, pp. 292–94.

LINDBLOM, JOH. *The Servant Songs in Deutero-Isaiah: A New Attempt to Solve an Old Problem.* Lund: C. W. K. Gleerup, 1951. P. 103.

——. *Prophecy in Ancient Israel.* Philadelphia: Fortress, 1963. Pp. 400–03, and esp. Additional Note VIII, pp. 428–30.

EICHRODT, WALTHER. *Theology of the Old Testament, Volume One.* Translated by J. A. BAKER. "The Old Testament Library." Philadelphia: Westminster, 1961. On p. 483, n. 4, the "corporate personality" theory is rejected.

DE FRAINE, J., S.J. *Adam and the Family of Man.* Translated by D. RAIBLEY, C. Pp. S. Staten Island, N. Y.: Alba House, 1965.

IN THE PSALMS

WEISER, ARTUR. *The Psalms: A Commentary.* Translation by HERBERT HARTWELL. Philadelphia: Westminster, 1962. See pp. 66–72, 80–81, and 91, on "laments of the individual" and the "I" of the Psalms.

NEW TESTAMENT APPLICATIONS

MANSON, T. W. *The Servant Messiah: A Study of the Public Ministry of Jesus.* Cambridge University Press, 1953. Pp. 73 f. Paperback reprint, 1961.

ROBINSON, JOHN A. T. *The Body: A Study in Pauline Theology* ("Studies in Biblical Theology," No. 5). Chicago: Henry Regnery, 1952. Pp. 55–67; cf. 14.

RUSSELL, D. S. *The Method and Message of Jewish Apocalyptic 200 B.C.–A.D. 100.* Philadelphia: Westminster, 1964. Pp. 132–39, 140 f., 153–57.

SHEDD, RUSSELL PHILIP. *Man in Community: A Study of St. Paul's Application of Old Testament and Early Jewish Conceptions of Human Solidarity.* London: Epworth, 1958; Grand Rapids: Eerdmans, 1964 (paper).